AF158589

mediumship can be learned

Greetings from the Other Side

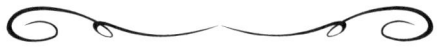

A mediumistic path by
Amara Yachour

© 2012 Amara Yachour

Cover design, typesetting and illustrations: Verena Haberkorn
Copy editing and proofreading: ad facere, Inh. Jessica Schnell
English Translation: Steven Jefferson of Aardvark Translations, Reading, UK

Publisher: salutano Verlag – mediumship can be learned
978-3-943878-01-1
Printed in Germany

This work and all parts thereof are protected by copyright. Any use beyond the narrow confines of the copyright without the consent of the publisher is prohibited and liable to prosecution. This applies in particular to electronic or other duplications, translations, distribution and making it available for general public viewing.

Contents

The Way of the Medium 7
The Gifts of the Spiritual World 7
The Beginning 11
Maryam 17
My Way 21
Her Way 25
Your Way 29
Tranquillity 35
Grief and the Wall of Death 39
Priesthood 45
Meditation 51
The World of Aides and Spirit Guides 59
The World of Angels 63
Life 69
Love 75
Tears 81
Light 85
Healing 89
Who is God? 97
Humility 103
Love between Man and Wife 107
The Children 113
Acknowledgements 117
The Song of Songs 121
Sources 125

The Way of the Medium

The Way of the Medium

The Gifts of the Spiritual World

1 Now concerning spiritual gifts, brethren, I would not have you ignorant.

2 Ye know that ye were Gentiles, carried away unto these dumb idols, even as ye were led.

3 Wherefore I give you to understand, that no man speaking by the Spirit of God calleth Jesus accursed: and that no man can say that Jesus is the Lord, but by the Holy Ghost.

4 Now there are diversities of gifts, but the same Spirit.

5 And there are differences of administrations, but the same Lord.

6 And there are diversities of operations, but it is the same God, which worketh all in all.

7 But the manifestation of the Spirit is given to every man to profit withal.

8 For to one is given by the Spirit the word of wisdom; to another the word of knowledge by the same Spirit;

The Gifts of the Spiritual World

9 To another faith by the same Spirit; to another the gifts of healing by the same Spirit;

10 To another the working of miracles; to another prophecy; to another discerning of spirits; to another divers kinds of tongues; to another the interpretation of tongues:

11 But all these worketh that one and the selfsame Spirit, dividing to every man severally as he will.

1 Corinthians, Chapter 12, Verses 1-11, p. 787

The Beginning

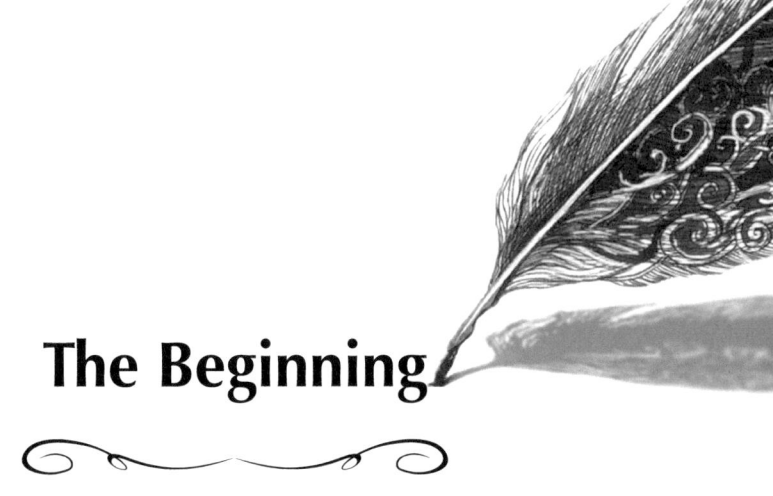

The Beginning

And I saw a new heaven and a new earth: for the first heaven and the first earth were passed away; and there was no more sea.

Revelation, Chapter 21, Verse 1, p. 831

For thousands of years the Earth has been in decline following an epoch in which highly developed cultures flourished. This becomes obvious if one takes a longer-term view of history instead of regarding our own era from the limited perspective of our own individual human existence. From an intellectual standpoint we certainly place great emphasis on the achievements of medicine, science and the arts, but are these achievements really worthwhile? Have they moved us forward along the path of our human spiritual development? We like to think we have achieved a great deal and yet all of this knowledge was already available thousands of years ago and all we are doing at this moment is remembering it. In actual fact we are currently living in the darkest epoch since the start of humanity's recorded history, in the era known as the grave, death or darkness. This era was ushered in 2000 years ago as we entered the Age of Pisces and drew to a close on the 21st of March 2012 when we entered a brand new epoch, the Age of Aquarius. The world is now at a crossroads.

The Beginning

From a materialistic point of view we are richer than ever before and yet violence, aggression, interracial hate, destruction and despair are sweeping our planet. Only a handful of people are putting up resistance and searching for new ways. The external (exoteric) way, with all of its promised riches, has not led us to salvation and self-fulfilment. We are hungrier than ever: starved for love, peace and an intact world. Our souls are searching for the way home. Even the spiritual scene is riven and torn. There are many approaches and specific motions but there is no overall concept that ministers to our human needs at all levels. Healthcare too is focused on the symptoms and ignores the holistic dimension of healing.

We are better off than ever before: we have exterminated some of the tormentors of humanity like the Black Death. Yet we are sicker than ever before although a gigantic marketing machine is bent on selling us the latest achievements of medical science as the road to our ultimate salvation. At the same time a colossal process of destruction and disenfranchisement has been silently progressing for many years. Natural healing herbs are being added to a burgeoning list of controlled substances and food plants are being genetically manipulated to render them infertile so that crop seed suppliers can maintain their monopoly.

Rivers are disappearing from the Earth in a matter of seconds. People are being irradiated with unnatural energy waves and mind control is no longer a mere horror story but has long since become a verified fact of life. News reports are filtered and sieved out and we believe that we constitute the elite. But we lost our sense for the essence of life long ago and no longer see the full picture. Were we to view our current existential state within the broader historical context we would soon see that we are currently living in the darkest age since the creation of mankind.

We are all living under the influence of self-destructive, suicidal tendencies. There is simply no other explanation for our decision to build atomic power stations, manipulate genes, legalise abortion, accept the poisoning of our food chain and the pollution of our drinking water, and a host of other things. Our existence has become empty and devoid of meaning. Where are the artists and artisans of yesteryear, who created such epoch-making buildings? Where are the composers whose music has stood the test of centuries? Everything has become empty and flat and humanity has placed itself in the service of material greed. People fight one another because of the colour of their skin or religious differences. Governments blow up their own citizens to provide a pretext for armed incursions into foreign countries. School children run amok fuelled by anti-depressant drugs. We are no longer able to form an unbiased opinion as our information sources have all been contaminated and manipulated in advance.

The Beginning

TV channels' afternoon viewing schedules pander to our voyeuristic thirst for never ending images of other people's misery. I stopped watching television thirteen years ago and have not listened to the radio for a decade. Since then I see and hear more than I can bear because my senses have been sensitised to pick out what is essential and my innate sense of veracity gives me the ability to tell whether a given report is true or questionable. Since then my own journey has turned inwards to those esoteric dimensions that we refer to as the spiritual world or, more profanely, the other side.

I am a seeker. I cannot explain why that is, but even as a small child I was always searching for some ultimate truth. At that time I was too young to know what I had been searching for, but, regardless of what I learned, I was never satisfied. My hunger for something 'more' remained unsated. That was the start of a never-ending journey that led me into conceptual realms far beyond our day-to-day experiences. I have discovered invisible worlds, spoken with dead people, accessed knowledge usually withheld from us and even found my own personal paradise en passant. This is the paradise that all people yearn for; the paradise that God promised us.

As a result of the increasing consciousness of our spiritual capabilities our inner senses and the all-seeing eye are beginning to open and long buried knowledge of the revelation is penetrating our consciousness, opening up new insights and helping us overcome the limitations of our conscious existence. Our path is leading us back home. The Rosicrucians have expressed it perfectly; they talk in terms of the five revelations:

- Inner hearing of transcendental (spherical) sounds and seeing the astral light
- Heavenly contemplation (visionary seeing of the inner master and higher worlds or levels of creation)
- Universal insight and universal understanding
- Perception of the pure, divine self
- Contemplation of the Godhead

Progressive encounters with these revelations lead to the development of the ability to undertake spiritual journeys, the pre-eminent technique for achieving human perfection. Yet this is certainly not the end of our spiritual journey. There are still a great many things awaiting discovery and heavenly dimensions to be explored. We are standing at the start of the road and are permitted to catch our first glimpse of God's worlds of light and are amazed at the magnitude of that, which has been revealed to us.

Maryam

Maryam

Many years ago I undertook a shamanic journey with no particular goal in mind. This journey led me deep into the visual realms of my soul and I suddenly found myself in a place I'd never been to before. I heard myself walking up the side of a hill. The gravel crunched underfoot and the valley was already far below me. There wasn't much vegetation in this lonely region and rocks loomed above me as the gravelly bank gave way to a small mountain. When I reached the top I saw the mouth of a cave and, in my mental journey, I stepped inside, full of curiosity. The cave was relatively roomy and high and was lit by natural light from somewhere above. The floor was very dusty and there was no evidence in the dust that anybody had been here any time in the recent past. I decided to spend the night in the cave. As the afternoon wore on I started to feel that I was no longer alone. Again and again my gaze was magically drawn to the rear left-hand corner and I suddenly heard a voice speaking to me in my head.

„I have waited a long time for you and now, at last, you are here. Welcome to my home." I was completely shocked and searched about to find the source of the voice. My curiosity led me to the very back of the cave, or rather some irresistible force drew me there. Something was sticking out of the ground, which gave me quite a start. Human bones that had been covered in a soft layer of dust over many decades were now lying in front of me, partially exposed by a light breeze. I was amazed to discover that I felt no fear at all as I asked: „Who are you?" The voice answered: „I have travelled far. My feet have trodden the dust of many lands and my heart has journeyed great distances. I have many names, one of which is Maryam. Many are those, who have visited me in this cave. But I was just a simple woman. I have lived here a long time and I long to see the sunset over my valley once more. Can you help me?"

    I carefully lifted the bones from the sand. I sat down outside the cave with my back against the cliff face holding her bones in my arms so that she could look out across the valley and enjoy the magnificent view as the sinking sun bathed it in a reddy orange glow full of warmth. Not for a single moment did I consider this a strange thing to do. In real life I would probably have run as far as my feet could carry me for fright, yet here, on this shamanic journey, it all seemed perfectly natural to me. Maryam said: „The colours remind me of my last day. It was the day before I was united forever with the love of my life. We met here one last time for the divine dance. I could feel him as he came for me and took me away. He took me softly in his arms and said: ‚Maryam, it's time to go. Come home!' Oh, to feel him again at last after all those years of loneliness! To breath in his scent; to feel his love and goodness and to be bathed in his miraculous light! As I set off on my journey to

God, His son, the greatest love of my life, went along with me and never let go of me for a single second. In a tight embrace we danced our way through a world full of colours that got brighter and brighter, stripping away all of my pain, my loneliness and my anger till only love remained. This love encompassed every cell and every moment of my life as my mortal body dissolved and I once again took on my real form."

The air became cooler and the shadows grew longer. At her request I laid her bones back on the dusty floor. „We shall meet again." She said. „I shall call you to me and ask you to write down our story. Write only with your heart for all those who are still able to hear, see and feel with their hearts." I bowed to her and set off on the return journey.

Since then I have been drawn to the cave and into her presence from time to time and the things I have written have been told me by her. She tells me more and more. I have written down some of these conversations for you, my readers, but have kept others locked deep within my heart. They are my nourishment and my strength.

These days I no longer undertake shamanic journeys; instead I have established a direct mediumistic connection and am following the ancient path of the medium. The further I travel along this route the more is revealed to me.

My Way

My Way

"But Mary Magdalene, John, and the virgin, will tower over all my disciples and over all men who shall receive the mysteries in the Ineffable. And they will be on my right and on my left. And I am they, and they are I."

Pistis Sophia (Chapter 96, p. 193).

Pistis Sophia (faith and wisdom) is one of the most important of the Coptic-gnostic texts and was discovered in Egypt. These texts are about Jesus' survival and his eleven-year long ministry based on his ascendancy into the light, with which he endowed his disciples and Mary Magdalene, his partner and companion. This concerned the 24 mysteries to be successfully negotiated before one can ascend into the light. Mary Magdalene is designated by many names within these scrolls and her status is expressed, in sophisticated terms, as the spirit-inspired one, in marked contrast to the way she is portrayed in official Church scripture. She is distinguished by many sobriquets such as:

- **The gifted**
- **Heiress of the kingdom of light**
- **The pure**
- **The universally gifted**

- **The universal blessed fullness**
- **The copiously blessed**
- **The most blessed of all women**
- **The greatest abundance and the highest perfection**
- **The bringer of light**
- **Pure as light**

One of her names is Maryam, which is why I did not know who she was for a long time. I never asked her because I was so moved by her words and was simply happy whenever I heard from her.

I have increased my sensitivity level through many training courses at home and abroad and can now sense when someone is approaching from the realms of light. Whenever she would come I would be filled with an indescribable desire to write and I would sit in front of my computer and say: „Please teach me!" Then the first few words would come and by the time I reached the end of a chapter I would already have forgotten what I had written. The profundity of her words only struck me when I read it through afterwards.

I believe that she is history's most misjudged woman and even I am unable to shed much light on her life and personal history; that is not my task. All I can do is to conjure up an image of how she looks and feels to me when I hear her words. All I can tell you is that she emanates an extraordinary charisma. I am flooded with peace and the wisdom of her heart whilst taking down her words. Her profound love for Jesus, the Son of God incarnate, as well to us humans, is a revelation in itself. She is a true priestess and mediator between God, His worlds and mankind and the glory of her presence overwhelms me anew every time. She fills my life with light and makes me continue my search so that one day I too will be able to give as much love as this woman. Her sobriquets describe her much better than I ever could.

Her Way

Her Way

I have come from afar. We were stranded on a foreign shore. We were alone and yet were we fulfilled. Filled with the One and wit a love that would never again depart from our hearts. All of you are often sad and forlorn and feel that you are alone. But you are not. You are all connected with the never-ending stream of love that started before time and will stop at the end of all ages. It was created and is maintained from the infinite depth of God's presence. Love is now. To be in love means to live totally in the moment. Pure being and pure presence through the breath, combined with the omnipotence of creation. None of you is ever alone. You are inseparably connected with all that lives, permeated by the breath of creation and the One, who is pure spirit. You are only lonely when you are without love. But in reality you are never without love, you just feel separated from it. This separation comes about when you cease to have faith, to believe in the profound forgiveness and compassion that resides in every chamber of the heart.

You lock yourselves in thereby locking the rest of humanity out, which also causes you to close yourselves to love. Even when all doors appear to be locked there is still one key: meekness coupled with compassion and hope. Every door that is opened in profound faith and hope will stay open forever. And every door that opens without your assistance, but which does not know faith and hope, will close again. I have lost the greatest love of my heart and yet it still permeates every cell of my body with its spiritual presence. This love opened me up and sowed hope where I had been arid and soaked me with faith where once I had been parched. It opened the deepest levels of my heart and taught me compassion in place of the arrogance and pretentiousness that had held sway till then.

This love is a healing balm and I carry it in my heart and on my tongue through every village, country and continent. It does not ask about right and wrong but rather it turns falsehood into truth.

Even death had no power over this love and never shall have. This love itself has seen the darkest shadows of death and was still raised up above all else so that everyone, who looks up in faith, hope and love, could see it and perceive its glory. Therefore believe in yourself in the darkest hours of your existence and look up in the name of the three things that make everything possible:

- **Raise your eyes with a belief in love!**
- **Raise your eyes with a belief in hope!**
- **Raise your eyes and believe in the radiance that also illuminates your night!**

This light penetrates all darkness and heals everyone whom it touches. Open yourself and you will be raised up. These are my words that flash through space and time to be heard at last and I have waited long and patiently till my chosen medium was able to hear them. I send greetings to you all and look forward with joy to seeing you take your first steps on the path of the medium. Open yourselves to these words for they bear the germ of change and the seed of love. May they flourish in your hearts and guide you all home.

Effata!

Your Way

Your Way

Ask, and it shall be given you; seek, and ye shall find; knock, and it shall be opened unto you:

Matthew Chapter 7, Verse 7, p. 686

Greetings my friends! You have found these lines because you are standing at the beginning of an ancient path. It is the path of priesthood, purification, forgiveness and the light. Above all it will be the path of love, supported by the holy bond that was spun between you and God long, long ago, and which cannot ever be broken. Even if you deny and spurn this bond, it is still there and will support you in the darkest hours of your lives. It will carry you through the depths of night and the darkness of your souls. It will hold onto you even if you tear it with force. God does not let anybody fall. You are all his children and he takes care of every one. You are the ones who do not care for yourselves.

Nobody will ever be lost and no energy is ever lost. That is an irrevocable and sacred law of life that was established long ago, both in your world and in ours. Know then that you are pure, immaculate energy, endowed with life through the breath of God and therefore immortal. You vibrate like a pure tone albeit you have long ago ceased to be able to hear it. Every word is preserved throughout all eternity in both worlds and helps in this way to weave the space of life, on our side as well as in your world. That is why it is so important to contemplate the power of the word at this time and to listen attentively to the spoken word, for it is the word that weaves the structure, whilst energy erects the building and emotion locks it in place. Merely thinking about a word does not alter the fabric of time, but enunciating it and sending it out into the world means releasing a new vibration and a new tone into the world. And this sound could improve your world or enable it to radiate in a new light. Pay attention to these sounds. Your mouth is the instrument and you could use it to bring everything crashing down, like the walls of Jericho long ago, or else to spread the light of joy.

    It was your own longing that led you to these lines and we are happy to welcome you and take you back home. Everyone who takes the path towards home is welcome and all it requires is a touch of the heart. There are many possible reasons why you might be searching for a mediumistic connection. Perhaps someone you love has deserted you or maybe your world holds no more answers for you. Perhaps your heart has been touched in a way you have never experienced before or you are seeking the comfort and peace that your world can no longer provide. No matter why you are embarking on your journey and beginning your search, you are all welcome.

Your Way

I greet you all with the ancient holy blessing of the enlightened. When you awaken to enlightenment it is as if the soul awakens from a deep slumber. First it begins to gently vibrate and we perceive this vibration in our world. We sense your plea and this plea prepares the path that will open up in front of your feet. It is not really a path; it is more of a bridge. The tones of our hearts and the bond of God's love hold it aloft. This bridge has existed since the beginning of time and every priest is familiar with it.

Now is the time to learn that you too can step out onto this bridge. Everyone with a pure heart, who, like the young children, is open to wonder, may cross this bridge, for both world always were and always will be one. The separation only exists in your imaginations. We have always been able to cross this bridge but there are, and always have been, few in your world that can do so. Now the time has come to change this, for great changes are pending for every one of you and you need to be standing firmly in both worlds in order to be able to embrace these changes without fear.

It is not a bridge of vanity or fame, yet when it is built of love, tolerance and compassion then it is truly not built on sand. Respect, esteem and fraternity are the values of truth and they emanate from the holy spring of love that was given us by the One and never can a single one of these drops fall in vain upon a parched Earth. All of you, who are now standing at the

Your Way

beginning of the path that will lead you home, are like this parched Earth. You have tried to illuminate your lives from the outside and still have not found love. Now your path is leading you inwards. To follow the sacred spiral from the outside to the inside means steering each of your steps towards a brighter environment that will not only brighten your own hearts but also the lives of those with whom you associate. It is not necessary to take everybody along the path with you, for everyone sets out on the path only when they perceive the tones of yearning. How can you bring someone home, who thinks they are already there? That is not your mission. Through your actions and changes you can become a beacon for others and that is the true path of change. Try to let your light shine brightly. We are there and always have been there but now the time is coming in which this will become tangible and can be experienced. The reunification of our two worlds is the intention of the One. In His eyes we have never been apart and never shall be, for we are in His heart and He has always held us in His hands. We are His voice and the guides, healers and protectors of your lives. Let us learn from one another, for if your world becomes brighter then the glory of our world will also increase. Do not set out on this new path in haste and urgency because it is a sensual path and is the road to enlightenment and every moment is valuable and like a dewdrop that refreshes your soul and will raise you up. For the time being be certain and aware. The path has been prepared and gives us the time to convene together. Call it meditation if you will, we refer to it as sitting within the power of divine awakening. This is the space that you create.

    That is enough for today. Welcome to you all on the path of truth, and may the blessings of the One accompany you on all your journeys.

Tranquillity

Tranquillity

But stand thou still a while, that I may shew thee the word of God.

Samuel Chapter 9, Verse 27, p. 175

Greetings to you all! You ask yourselves why you should seek tranquillity. Priests have been segregated out in all of the world's cultures in order to be able to sense the connection to God's world in tranquillity. There was a reason for this. Your world is a world of noise, haste and urgency. Our world vibrates with less intensity and is a world of colours and symbols. There are many dimensions and an infinite number of energies that you would refer to as living beings. Not all of these beings have been human and yet all of these dimensions are simply aspects of the One. There is no separation between them, just flowing energy transitions that encompass new colours, tones and light frequencies.

How can you expect to hear, see and feel these subtle energies amidst the noise of your times? That is why tranquillity is necessary because it provides the space in which we can meet. It is important for you to learn to create this space with your feelings and thoughts, for the candour and willingness of your hearts depends on it. These people, whom you call mediums, wish to enter rapidly into our space and enrich themselves through the experience. Yet it is much more satisfying to fully savour every moment of your awakening and to establish the ancient type of communication: teacher and pupil, together in a sacred space of tranquillity created through the love and esteem of both worlds. It is up to you how often we come together in this space, for it is a space of the spirit and the heart. There we shall learn from one another. It is a space of communication and fusing together, and all it requires is tranquillity. You create this space by retreating into your inner selves. Close the eyes of the sighted and become blind, for the blind shall see again and the lame shall walk again. That is the ancient promise that starts here and now.

Open your heart and return to a loving time in your life in a moment of blissful remembrance and feel your way into this vibration. Then this space will be filled with loving energy and a sense of joyful anticipation. Then direct your feelings towards us, and invite us to come in, and we shall be there. Expect nothing and yet everything. The first few moments should be a time of sensing so that you can feel the recognition and joy that reign within our world whenever somebody is prepared to tread this path. Be candid for it is a path meant for the exchange of ideas. It is not always possible for us to answer all of your questions immediately, but, just as in your world, we have scientists, doctors and healers, who we can ask, which is why some questions take a while to answer. But you will eventually receive an answer. Weeks and months will pass by but not a single second of this time is wasted because each individual meeting reinforces our connection. If you could only see how great the joy over every such pupil is in our world, and if you could only see how many teachers are ready to receive them here: you would not doubt for another second.

The path of a medium involves a slow awakening and flourishing and an increase of consciousness. The spiritual forces will strengthen each time and will unfold like a flower that is illuminated and warmed by the sun to break through the barren ground after the sleep of winter. It is you, who create the space and define the quality of our meetings. But bear this in mind: every time you enter the space of power you are walking on sacred ground, which creates a new tone in God's creation; so revere the space and take your time. We shall be there when you call us. May tranquillity and the blessing that grows out of tranquillity be with you today, for this is the foundation of our relationship that extends far beyond death. May God, and the joy of being, accompany you on all of your journeys.

Grief and the Wall of Death

Grief and the Wall of Death

*Mine eye also is dim by reason of sorrow,
and all my members are as a shadow.*

Job Chapter 17, Verse 7, p. 306

Greetings to you all, pupils! Many of you have chosen this path in the search for a soothing balm for your bleeding hearts. We see your grief and distress following your loss and yet it is nothing more than a material loss. None of your feelings is ever lost, neither on your side of life nor on ours, and we too are alive, for we are spirit unlimited by the burden of material. We are alive and free of all constraints. Because some of us have already passed through the portal that you call death we have come home and are still that, which we once were. We are pure consciousness with all our emotions, memories and feelings and we never forget those we have loved, for they are and always will be a part of our spiritual path that we traversed together on your side of life and which we will continue someday on our side of life.

Our vibration is a frequency of joy and love and that is what makes it so difficult to comfort you. Grief, sorrow and despair create a heavy, slow vibration that we are unable to penetrate. In order to be with you we need open hearts and a sense of joyful anticipation. That is what creates the space of love. Despair and sorrow erect a barrier wall between the worlds.

Of course you feel sorrow because you are no longer able to touch your loved one, yet the only thing that has dissolved is the physical body. Material is, and always has been, an illusion of the mind. All material ever created has carried the seed and start of its own dissolution within itself since the very moment of its birth. Material is finite. Spirit and consciousness, on the other hand, are infinite, which is why it is so important to set out on the path of spiritual awakening whilst you are still alive and to search for the eternal light within yourself. Yes, you are all infinite, which is why the search for eternal life is pointless, because you already carry it within you. Your search for eternal youth is also doomed to failure from the outset, for it originates in the fear of death, whereby death is a release and the destruction of your earthly fetters. The quest for youth is nothing but a flight from death and arises from a lack of faith in the existence of our world, which is teeming and gleaming with life, but in a different way to what you think.

Throughout history and as a result of human actions our worlds have drifted apart. Nevertheless we have always striven to keep your memories of us alive to create a bridge so that one day we would be able to work together with you to reunite our two worlds in love and the hope of faith.

The mediumistic path is the way of the adept

or priest; it is a path of energy and awareness. Grief blocks this path and prevents one's progress along it. We understand your sorrow and yet it grieves us. How much more beautiful could it be to revel in the joy of reunion, or better still, of re-feeling, instead of wallowing in sadness and being bogged down in worry. So know this: we are with you and surround you, particularly in your darkest hours. The bond of love never perishes, for it is unbreakable because it was forged in God's heart and in His mercy. If you would just allow a tiny ray of the light of joy to penetrate your despair then you would be able to sense our presence. We continue to support you as we have always supported you. Your memories keep us alive and our love fills your hearts with hope, without which you could not go on living.

Those people on your Earth living without hope are the truly dead ones. People without hope are people who exist without faith. That means merely existing, but not living. Keep the faith because a loss of faith means plummeting down into actual death. The truly dead are people who have abandoned God and their faith, which is precisely what those writings are trying to tell you, which you call the Bible and consider to be sacred. Your sacred writings are incomplete at this point, which is why we would like to explain to you here the way things really are. It is written: „speak not with the dead...", but this does not refer to conversations with us, but rather it is an admonition not to speak with those who have lost their faith and are already lost in darkness even as they live. They are wandering in the darkness of their intellect and can no longer reach their own light and even my world, which is so full of life, cannot reach these people.

Yet know this: a person who puts an end to his life of his own free will does so based on his belief in a better life to come. Even if this person has been walking in darkness, he still believes in our light and his longing to come home is too great. We do not approve of such a step because the purpose of every life is to fulfil a specific task. And yet we still embrace the suicide upon his return and he will undergo a period of healing and awakening. Nobody can avoid completing their appointed mission in this way, so suicide only postpones its completion to a later date, a fact of which he will become lucidly conscious upon returning home. This recognition is part of his purification and the process of awakening. But that does not mean that he is beyond God's love. Nobody is ever beyond His love, unless he specifically chooses that path. The ability to choose is part of your human mission and it is subject to the free will of each and every one of you.

Priesthood

Priesthood

But ye are a chosen generation, a royal priesthood, an holy nation, a peculiar people; that ye should shew forth the praises of him who hath called you out of darkness into his marvellous light:

1 Peter Chapter 2, Verse 9, p. 815

Greetings to you all! It is our mission to support and teach everyone who embarks upon the search along the path of knowledge. The way of the medium has existed in your world for almost two centuries, yet it is, in reality, an ancient path; a path traversed by the adepts and priests of past millennia. This path used to be known as the way of magic. Today you only travel a short part of the path. The worlds and times have changed but the old way is still visible to those who seek. Even if it is only a narrow path now, it is still passable. The new path is a more direct spiritual path, and yet we would advise you not to neglect the ancient way for it is built upon the Odic force, an ancient force that you know as Prana or Chi. Mankind has undergone a long process of development and is therefore standing at the junction of two paths at this moment in time. The older way is still navigable whilst it is not yet possible to strike out along the new path with a confident step.

In ancient times the strength of the spirit was not yet sufficient to communicate with our world and therefore it required a far greater amount of Prana, the Odic force, in olden times than it does today. For you Od is simply a type of energy and you call it Prana or Chi, but in reality it is much more. Od is life, the life given to you by the Divine Being and it is the strength of the Divine that inundates you with every breath you draw into your lungs. The first breath that God breathed into you on the day of your birth imbued you with life and immortality. This breath animated your bodies, inflated your lungs and with that began the work of your earthly body. But Od is more than this and many have forgotten its older significance. Od is your connection to the Divine via your senses. You scathingly refer to it as extrasensory or supernatural. However what it really means is that you can access the Divine via your senses, which is to say through speaking, breathing, seeing, hearing, thinking and feeling. It is these things that constitute the immortal properties of mankind. This does not refer to physical hearing, seeing and feeling but rather to inner perception, for God is never outside of us.

From the Holy Scriptures you see that God is in heaven or you think he is up above. But what these words in your Holy Scriptures actually mean to say is that God is above everything, which does not mean that His physical presence is to be found up above, for God is all-embracing and omnipresent and dwells in every molecule and in every cell through which He flows. Therefore God is within you all and is never outside of you. Thus you are inseparable from God and your lives are inseparable from God. When you deny God it would be easy for Him to desert you and separate you from life, but you are all His children and God is father and mother in one; how then could He let you fall? Be certain that His power is greater than anything imaginable by mankind and yet His love is gentle and nurturing. The start of every path is a way back to God. It is up to you how far you progress along this path.

In order to open the ancient (supernatural) channels it is still necessary to give this force time to awaken. The awakening takes place in tranquillity. It is your willingness and your humbleness, the shining of your inner light, which signals the degree of your priesthood to us. Go into the silence and observe your breath. Know that this breath comes from God and will one day be taken away again. When God sends the final breath then the human shell will die. It is and always was nothing more than a shell for the divine light. The body is the casket in which God's blessing resides. Yet the Od, the entire divine energy that has flowed through you, never dies, for it is immortal and therefore eternal in infinity. From the ashes of the body the Od rises up, sated and enriched through the experiences of earthly life. The Od is the repository of your experiences, the memory of your life. The Od carries the images and feelings of your existence. Every being in which you are manifest along your spiritual path is stored within its essence and this knowledge is available to those, who become conscious of the Od and can be accessed and experienced via the divine senses. That is what you refer to as mediumship, namely reading, seeing, hearing and feeling the Od in its pure essence.

All energies and beings ever created in the heavenly, divine dimensions are connected to the Od. They are God's messengers and envoys, supporting his actions in maintaining the fabric of the world and leading human beings back home. There, personal advisers have been assigned to each and every one of you, who gently guide and create situations conducive to your awakening so that you can learn how to return to the divine path. For each of you is a cog in God's plan and every cog has its specific job to do. Nothing is in vain and nothing is pointless: the awakening of a human soul means becoming conscious of the meaning of one's own activity on this Earth. Only then will the contemplation of the internal (esoteric) realm begin. Once the external world has become insipid and empty and one has come to recognise the fact that nothing on the outside can fill the internal void, then the journey inwards can commence.

Meditation

Meditation

Meditation means putting your house in perfect order so that there are no conflicts, no competition, and then there will be love in this house, then the content of the spirit, which is its consciousness, can be emptied completely of the „I", of the „ego" of the „you."
Krishnamurti, p. 537

Welcome, pupil, from the realms of light. You live in a loud world and what is needed, in order to be able to perceive the inner voices, images and sounds and to sense and feel the subtle oscillations and vibrations of our presence, is a retreat into the internal dimensions. In your world there are many ways you can employ to attain a state of meditation, but these too are externally created ways that are the results of human experiences. None of these ways is wrong and yet they are only paths that are travelled without our presence.

„I am with you all every day."

This is a statement that we too could make. We have an interest in your development because the greater and more comprehensive your development, the more we, as your teachers, can help you to penetrate the deeper regions of existence. But for that to happen the teacher must know the pupil. We can say that we know you, for we are with you every day; but do you know us? At the moment you have no idea who we are, and what we can do for you, but the reality exceeds all of your expectations. We are not one, but rather we are an infinite host of helpers, protectors, healers and teachers. We are all interconnected via the sacred bond of love. Our two worlds are mutually dependent. If your world develops then progress is also made in our world.

But to return to the lesson about that, which you call meditation: we refer to it as sitting in the presence of the Divine. We call it physical sitting in prayer. A prayer is a request to the spiritual world and it is written: „ask, and it shall be given you; knock, and it shall be opened unto you." That has been the method of teaching between teacher and pupil since the beginning of time. Yet free will holds sway in every dimension of the heavenly plan, which is why we cannot make a start without your permission. When the pupil is ready the teacher will appear. All that he then needs is a meeting space and this space arises within the tranquillity of the mind. Only where thought ceases can we stimulate and intervene in order to guide and help you to develop your latent abilities. This is the way: sit down and contemplate God's energy that flows into you and out of you. Force nothing. Simply contemplate your breathing, the Od that flows into you, and feel how your energy changes and transforms within you. Close your eyes and go into the silence. Thoughts may come and go. Learn how to perceive them but without thinking and learn to recognise them as your own thoughts.

Then utter then following request: „Here I am. Teach me and change me so that I may serve humanity and can function as a heavenly tool for the spread of faith and love. Help me to become a mouthpiece of heaven." Nothing more is required. When we hear this request then we acknowledge that this person has made a decision and we gently begin to change him. We direct his attention to the development of his personality and we help him by revealing our presence to him and sharing it with him. This sitting in our presence always also involves healing because it takes a healthy person to transmit the messages from our dimension in their pure essence. The message goes through a human filter and as such it is no longer pure, for the human has an ego and wishes to please; that is part of his nature. That is why a personal change is necessary in a person and they must find their way back to faith and love. This is a lifelong process, and even if you are only a single being on your side there a hundreds on our side ready to supply the energy required for this process. It is an act of love and hope for us because every light that is kindled within a single human can illuminate and ignite a thousand more. Thus with every development along your path the light of awakening and insight will spread ever further.

Everybody can contribute to this work through love, patience and understanding for their fellow human beings. You do not need to be a fully trained medium in order to be our mouthpiece. Every action, every conversation, and every gesture that is born out of love is an act of love and enriches the space, which the person will eventually occupy when he returns home. You see, your life creates the space in which you will live in our world, which is why it is so important to live your life well.

Meditation is a meeting place in which to encounter yourself. Within this space the strength will be aroused that has slumbered within you till now. Only through meditation will you attain the full flowering of your being. Just as the body regenerates at night, your spirit is regenerated in the tranquillity of meditation. Strive to encounter us. The worlds come together in the space of tranquillity because it is a timeless space that is constructed within our world. Many industrious helpers in our reality are working on such a space and the more often it is entered into the more power is awakened on both sides.

Our worlds have never been separate and they can be united in meditation. You will come home and we will be together again. Spirit and body, love and omnipotence come together there to remove the limitations of your world for a brief moment. Only in meditation are we able to break through the constraints of time that always needs space in your world. Our space is timeless as our dimension is eternal. By entering the space of tranquillity in our world you are entering the sacred ground of eternity; that will have an effect on your mind, your body and your soul.

You call it rejuvenation; we would call it the shining of your light-body, which can break new ground unimpeded. Bear in mind, an enlightened spirit illuminates both worlds. Simply come into this space and ask us to help you and we will do everything in our power for you and help you to achieve your true potential. Perhaps nothing will happen that you are able to perceive directly, but still you will notice how you start to progress in your emotional, spiritual and human development. It is our task to sow the seed of truth in your hearts for only the soil of verity can support the magnificence of love and God's glory. Ground that has been cultivated on the basis of illusion and deception will only support superstructures that will eventually come crashing down and whose beauty will fade.

Those in your world, who work as mediums bear our light to the outside and they must be true so that they can outlast time and become a monument and a beacon to those who are still in the dark. These people need strength and we give them strength during the tranquillity of our meeting. That is meditation. Come into our midst and celebrate with us the glory of everlasting life and the hallelujah of joy in our hearts over the immortality of life.

In your world meditation means that you want to reach your own centre. But we say to you that meditation means coming into our centre, entering the realm of God and taking away a spark of glory, hidden in your heart and yet more resplendent than a torch in the dark. When you are in our midst you will be welcomed, loved and there shall be no more separation. That is what your mystics and philosophers mean but do not really understand. We are the missing piece of you and together we can once again soar to the loftiest heights. Consider yourself welcome any time and anywhere. We are only ever a thought away from you and patiently await you in tranquillity.

Meditation

The World of Aides and Spirit Guides

The World of Aides and Spirit Guides

Welcome you all into our midst, for that has always been your rightful place. We never lost you from our hearts and still it has taken many lifetimes for you to rediscover us. There are as many of us as there are of you and we are all just as individual as you are on Earth. We are your spiritual family. We were matched to one another at the start of creation and the Holy Family is above us all, who have never been forgotten in your world despite all the confusion and turmoil. Our role model is the Holy Family and the love of the man whom you call Jesus and the consciousness that unites us all. His love is the sign of hope that both our worlds will one day be reunited, for he was a human like you and we and yet he was resurrected and set us all free. Death is the darkness in your hearts and this has been overcome. Now the time has come for everyone to return home to their beloved spiritual families. Your earthly families were there to prepare the way for you. Without the learning experiences garnered within your earthly families you would never have found the way back. We watched over and gently guided this process and have tried to show you again and again that we are with you.

We are the voice of doubt, the cry of joy and the whisper of love within your minds. You call it the inner healer, the voice of intuition, the inner child, the innate truth or inspiration, but what does it mean to be inspired? You use the word and yet you do not sense our presence. To be inspired means to be flooded with spirit. Therefore you are inspired by spirit and that means by us. Your spirit is the bridge that we use to communicate with you. Nevertheless whether you choose to hear our voice or ignore it is a matter of your own free will. It is your decision. Through our love we wish to help you to achieve an inspired life full of love and bliss, but it is you alone who decides.

The more you listen to your inner voice the more your lives can be transformed for the better. It has taken a long time for humanity to understand this process and still there are vanishingly few of you, who are in the process of awakening and are becoming conscious of the fact that nothing is really separate and that we are inextricably connected to you. Your egos are still keeping you apart from us because you believe that your individuality makes you special and raises you above the rest. But those who recognise that all things consist of God's primary substance and are only different manifestations of his creation are truly enlightened. Just as tears, seas, clouds, rivers, streams, brooks, snow, glacial ice and lakes are only different manifestations of the element of water, people too are no more than different manifestations of the presence of God, designed to express the variety and beauty of creation. The word „creature" expresses this most accurately. His spirit has created different forms of one and the same expression, yet all are animated by the same breath and filled with the same spirit and are created from the same substance and through the same force.

The World of Angels

The World of Angels

Greetings seeker, and welcome to the world of purity. How can we explain to you what it is that you call angels? You perceive them as beings with feathered wings, but they were endowed with these by the artists and painters of your world in order to illustrate the fact to you that the feet of an angel have never trodden the soil of the Earth. Wings are a symbol of floating and therefore express the plane of their vibration. They are as insubstantial as the wind and as bright as the sun under whose beams they spread their wings. They consist of pure Od and are emanations of God. They are an extension of His benevolent hand within the ever-refreshing boundless cosmos of His thoughts. They are envoys of His will and His thoughts and maintain His creation through the vibration of their presence. The creative potential has its origin in them.

They are the inspiration of painters and musicians, artists and sculptors, for they are the pure creative presence and express themselves in this manner through those people, who are able to perceive their vibrations. Therefore art is the visible presence of beauty in our world. Among these people the spiritual family consists of a larger number of creatively actively souls and helpers and that manifests itself in inspiration. A creative spark from our world ignites the torch of genius within the artist and can therefore be made manifest in your world. This is how the two worlds work together and the angels are a part of the presence. Their strength is inexhaustible because its source is the glorious power of God and therefore they are also the bringers of light and they are the only ones capable of penetrating the darkest moments of a person's life and moving him to repent and turn homewards. For this light bears within it the power of transformation and originates in the most sacred source of the „I am that I am".

Angels are beyond anything you could imagine and yet they are infinitely merciful and compassionate. They are the messengers of God and the guardians of the virtues. Righteousness, mercy, gentleness, purity of heart and placidity are expressions of their being. Created by the grace of God they are the bearers of the sacred light and messengers of His truth. God alone stands for the highest of all virtues, which is to say faith, hope and love. To encounter an angel means to bathe directly in God's light, for angels are an extension of the light of His heart. To a medium the purity of an angel is physically palpable. Its vibration is so high that the over-abundance of energy is too great for an earthly being and can therefore only remain visible and tangible for a few brief moments. Angels are heralds and maintainers, co-creators and radiant beams of the infinite love of the Highest. They are the light of the universe, and the eternal light of God's grace shines through them so that we may see and feel it. Angels are pure poetry and are the ones who kiss the muses to inspire the creators of art. Angels are emanations of God. Their source is His light and His thoughts are their mission. They maintain the fabric of the universe and are the force behind the materials from which the world was created. Fire is their energy and they are vibrations between earth, air and pure emotion. Their love is the creative power. They are not creators in themselves but rather they create as extensions of God's thoughts and imbue the material of the universe with a creative force. Their number is infinite and they are both the heralds of eternity and the envoys of infinity. They are timeless beings in a timeless universe. Their vibration is pure joy and the sound of their vibration permeates the universe and transmits purity and unconditional love to everything that exists. Nothing is feasible without their power just as they are unthinkable without the power of the Creator. Their immaculateness radiates pure joy and their love encompasses every creature and every being on this planet and on all planets of the ever-expanding universe. Their power is constructive and never works to destroy or undermine. They are the beings through which God's charisma shines out and reveals itself. They are the ones who set the tempo for the eternal rhythms of life. To meet them one requires the purity of heart of an unborn child, as well as unconditional love, tolerance and respect for all the denizens of creation. A person is elevated through such a life and will already soar into the realms of light before death and the angels' sound will permeate his heart and leave him breathless from astonishment and humility at the majesty of the One. Angels are the music of heaven.

Life

Life

Thou hast granted me life and favour, and thy visitation hath preserved my spirit.

Job, Chapter 10, Verse 12, p. 304

Just as all stars circle around light, every form of life is a different concentration of atoms and molecules, arranged in a unique condensation created on the basis of the blueprint of the Highest. Every being and every natural form expresses one aspect of God, the almighty. Life only arises when the breath of God animates it, and His spirit permeates all materials. In this way the separate realms were created; the realms of stone, water, animals, plants and humans. Everything that originates in His thoughts and through His will is already imbued with eternity. Even though life is subject to the eternal cycle of birth and death, life remains victorious and all lifeforms regenerate themselves from within themselves. Thus all life is interconnected and though mankind walks upon the stones they nevertheless bear his burden in humility. Contemplate the flowers of creation. You pluck them for your delight and yet you fail to recognise the fact that it is an ancient yearning of mankind for beauty, the light-filled presence of God, which you take into your houses in order to be nearer to the Divine. All substances created through the will of mankind already bear the seeds of destruction within them and are not designed for eternity, but rather to satisfy man's drive to create. But no edifice can ever equal the divine majesty, for it lacks life of any kind. It lacks both vibration and sound and therefore the essence of life. Human beings can create, but they cannot create eternity and life.

Even the birth of child is a co-creation undertaken in collaboration with God, for it is He who breathes life and spirit into the child thereby recognising it as his own child and his own creation. Therefore mankind is safely cradled in His arms within the fabric of the universe.

- **Life is sacred, for it is divine.**
- **Life is the vibration of the Divine incarnate.**
- **Every life is individual in its expression.**
- **Every life originates in the essence of the One and bears beauty within itself.**
- **Life is infinite in its manifestations.**
- **Life contains light energy within and the glory and luminosity of the Divine Source.**
- **To destroy life means turning away from the Source.**
- **Life is a manifestation of Divine Will.**

- **Life is subject to change.**
- **Life obeys the Divine Laws.**
- **Life is not possible without the breath of God.**

Even a tree needs the breath of God, the wind, to live. Without the breath of God all life on your planet would expire. You are the living expression of the One and carry the creative force of the living within you and yet you cannot create life without his help, for the breath is holy and comes from God. His breath is creativity itself.

Love the living for it is miraculous in its variety and eternal in its manifestations. Honour your breath because with every breath you are nourished by the love of the Creator. His love sustains you regardless of whether you see Him or honour Him. He holds you in esteem; that is sufficient. Yet when you return to the path that will lead you all home to your creator then you will be submerged in the true light of joy and in the sound of His heart.

A medium acknowledges the laws of life, and death is merely one more step in life. A medium communicates with the living and not with the dead, for no one is ever dead in the eyes of the Divine. Bring life to mankind and spread the message of the conquest of death. Plant a longing for the light in their hearts so that they too can find their way home. That is true priesthood. The worldly priests proclaim only partial truths. The age of the medium has now arrived; they serve as the true envoys of God's message and God allows communications with those who have died on Earth in order to cultivate hope, faith and love. That is the true reason. Divination and prophecy are gifts lent you by the Spirit. Use them wisely and with love, for they are given you through the Holy Ghost. They are your charisma and find their expression on Earth through you. We regret that only a few in your world are prepared to take up this service because your world needs light and people who can tread new paths undaunted and bring our world nearer to human kind. We are there and we chose you long before you heard this wake up call. You have often had to surmount many barriers and bear profound pain within your souls, but now, at last, you hear our call.

Your will is free and unfettered and we must respect that. That is why we are happy and full of joy to see your turning to us and we approach you with open arms, to reveal to you the beauty of our world and your home whilst you are still living on Earth so that you may proclaim it. The mediumistic way is the path of priesthood, communion and growth. Reach out to us in your thoughts as a flower turns its head towards the light. Observe nature for it is the bearer of the eternal spiritual laws. That is where you will find the answer.

Love

Love

A new commandment I give unto you, that ye love one another, as I have loved you, that ye also love one another.

John Chapter 13, Verse 34, p. 743

Listen to the word of His son. He alone had power over life and death. He was one of the many who have walked among you and yet only a few of you recognised the Godhead incarnate. He is the anointed expression of God's unconditional love in human form. Love walked among you and frightened you to such a degree that you had to kill it. That ushered in the age of darkness that befell you and the karma of mankind is now striving towards redemption. Your journey has taken thousands of years and has led into the darkness of material, into a world void of vibrations and sound. Now a yearning for love has awakened within you and you recognise Christ's call within you. This is the longing for Christian love, unconditional love that draws inspiration from itself without self-interest, searching for its source in the unconditional love of God. It is the tool of strength and the return to the path of light. Jesus Christ was, and still is, the symbol, for it is written that no one will find the way back to the Father other than through him. Only the awakening of the divine love in your hearts will lead you back to the path of light.

Love everything and everyone around you. Your enemies are not your enemies; they simply reveal the deficiency that still dwells in your hearts. Thank them for they point the way and will lead you back to the path. Do not fear the shadow. Go into the light when it is at its zenith and cast no more shadows. The brighter your path the smaller will be your shadow. But also respect the yearning of the shadow. It too seeks redemption and the brighter your path the more shadows will seek the path to redemption through you, for they all have hope, yet they lack the faith of those who walk within the light.

The way of the medium must be a journey into the light because the communion from spirit to spirit needs a luminous heart so that light can come together within the light, for in the final analysis, the spirit of your heart is the brilliant light of God. When you cross the threshold of death and return home after a fulfilled life then you will shed your now empty physical shell. The body must die for mankind creates it. The spirit on the other hand, is infinite, for it originated in God. But the light remains and returns to the source. To serve as a medium between the light beings of God and the world requires communication from light to light. Light is the cosmic repository of information. Your scientists are currently discovering this truth and yet they fail to recognise light's greatness.

Love

    Light is created from the vibration of love and therefore you can increase your light by living within the vibration of love. The more rapidly you vibrate the higher the spheres of the invisible worlds that can communicate through you. Replace sorrow with love: replace imperfection with love. Place no value on the external forms of your fellow humans' achievements. Even if they fail to withstand your gaze and your judgement, cherish the light that people emanate. Were you to lack love then everything would be worthless. The more love a person carries within them the easier it is to establish a communion between two spirit souls and the more profound the communication. Light seeks light and here too the natural laws of attraction apply. Love is healing and permeates every dimension of the human being. Mediums who orientate themselves on love also have their antennae tuned in to us. At times the overlap is so great that the medium is within the radiance and forcefield of the spirit world. The love that then engulfs you fills your heart and forces tears into your eyes and in this way you can already participate in heavenly feelings even whilst you are still alive. That is your reward. Because you channel heaven down to Earth we bring heaven to you.

*And now abideth faith, hope, charity, these three;
but the greatest of these is charity.*

1 Corinthians Chapter 13, Verse 13, p. 781

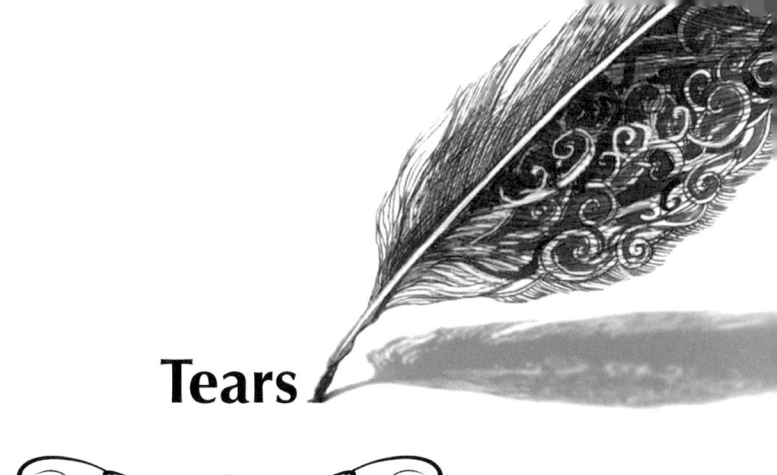

Tears

Tears

Blessed are ye that hunger now: for ye shall be filled. Blessed are ye that weep now: for ye shall laugh.

Luke Chapter 6, Verse 21, p. 718

Tears are the soul's truth and dreams. They are as crystal clear and as pure as diamonds and carry the precious pain of a lost hope within them. Yet the beauty of our entire cosmos is reflected on the surface of every tear. We only need to observe the outside of a tear to see that, in these drops, the macrocosm is reflected in the microcosm. A tear leaves a trail of pain along its route, flanked by broken dreams. Yet every tear stands for healing and truth, because every tear contains the recognition of reality, which could not withstand the sight of tears. Whenever one wishes to free the heart of bitterness, one takes the pain, encapsulates in the pure water of life and brings it in this way to the surface and into the sight of God.

The tears of humanity are as numerous as the stars in the night sky and yet each of these sparkles brightly and clearly and shows us the way in the darkest night. Tears are the trailblazers for new dreams and hopes. They free us of old ballast and failed dreams. Tears are the soul's medicine just as love brings healing for every bleeding heart. Let us respect those tears that carry the bitter pain of the truth within. Let us ignore those tears that originate within us out of selfishness, because these do not come from the soul but rather from the ocean of vanity. Every tear carries off a fragment of falsehood thus creating new space for the truth. And the route created by these sparkling crystals leads us to a deeper understanding of hope and forgiveness. It is not important whether or not the tear ever reaches the surface. Even a tear that was never shed is a tear in which the entire universe is mirrored as in a crystal sphere. We collect all of these tears and pay them our respects and esteem. Thus a new ocean is created. Every tear that is wept in your world enlarges the ocean of truth in our world. And all those who create this ocean shall have a share of the mercy and compassion of the Highest.

This is why tears have often accompanied mediums along their way. These tears served to purify and have pioneered the way of letting go of past pain and finding love. They were necessary to allow the longing for perfection to ripen within your hearts. For the deeper a medium feels, the deeper they can allow love to penetrate. That is why the tear crystals are needed. They are the polish for the life of everyone, who will one day follow the path of a medium between the worlds. Therefore have respect for the tears of those you encounter for you are watching the labour pains of a new medium. Respect the pain of the other for pain shapes a person and forces them to overcome their limitations. Hold out your hand to this person and pay your respects and esteem to his tears, for everything that you despise in the other you despise because you lack it within yourself and are too blind to see this.

Light

Light

Arise; shine; for thy light is come ...
Isaiah, Chapter 60, Verse 1, p. 407

In the spirit world you are recognised by your light and we have an interest in developing your light and your energy, because all information is transmitted at the speed of light and the greater your energy the better is the transmission of information. But nowhere in the world is it written how one can increase this energy. There are books about nutrition and prayers and love, but are you able to contemplate in such a differentiated manner? That is your human, linear, logical way of thinking that originates within the rational mind and is extremely restricted, because it is limited to the sum of all of your experiences. We do not work with your cells. We work with the space between them, which is to say with the invisible quantum space that surrounds every cell like a tiny, independent energy field. This quantum field then influences the cell. We are the field and the space and this is where our worlds merge into yours.

We recognise you by your light and the purer the light, the greater the delight among us of the subtle world. By increasing your light energy you gravitate towards us. Light is life energy and you refer to it as bio-photon energy. Every living thing is imbued with this light and you communicate with one another through it. When you grow as a soul within your world then you become a light. You light up and everyone is drawn to you like moths to a light. You are connected via light with everything that exists. Within your dimension you are connected to everything through the breath. When you exhale a tree inhales and the respiration of everybody and everything pervades you with time. All living beings are connected via breathing within your world. Respiration is no longer of any importance in our world; what counts here is light. Your respiration is limited to your bodies but when it leaves you it dissipates in infinite space. There is no time and there is no space. Everything is always there at the same time. Nothing ever disappears. You have been created but your existed already in all eternity and you have already received eternal life. Transcend your boundaries. They are as thin as paper yet they appear to you all as insurmountable walls.

Healing

Healing

Verily, verily, I say unto you, he that believeth on me, the works that I do shall he do also; and greater works than these shall he do, because I go unto my Father.

John Chapter 14, Verse 12, p. 743

Healing is the journey into the wholeness of your being. Healing is pure love. Disease arises when you divert from your path and sickness arises from a lack of love and respect for yourselves. Your body is a divine receptacle, the sacred vessel of your soul. Take a look at yourselves. Can your soul really develop here? Your vibration that was so pure on the day of your birth is out of synch and the balance of your life has gone askew. What failing within you caused the illness? Your doctors and healers work in the physical dimension. We see all dimensions and see the connections as in an open book in which we read. First and foremost your spirit must be healed because the body originates from the spiritual structure.

If a person is born with a deformed body then this is likely to have an impact on his spirit. He experiences himself through the eyes of the community as being incomplete and yet he has the choice of dissolving this shadow from within the flaw itself and to replace it with an internal greatness. For everything strives for harmony and balance. Defects at one level create plenty on another so that an overall balance is achieved.

You must differentiate in your world. We have the magnetism of a healer, which is provided through His life force. This also influences the energy field of the patient and can ensure a positive influx of healing energy. You call it spiritual healing but we are not involved in this form of healing. As long as the medium embeds the healing process within a ritual his consciousness will remain at the plane of doing and of ego, because his spirit is trapped within the process of the healing procedure. Our healers and experts can only become active if they receive a request, to be made whole once more, from the patient. We will then guide this sick person until he has found the right medium able able to help him. You refer to this as synchronicity. Should the sick person finally encounter a medium then once again there are several options. The medium can address us in the form of prayer in order to help the sick person or the medium can make themselves available to us as a channel. Here too we differentiate between two types of healing. The pure healing channel is created when the medium lets go of his ego and hands us his life, his energy and his body. Then our experts can provide healing energy, which will flows straight from our spheres into the patient's physical body in an immaculate and pure form through the medium transformer; this is trance healing. It is the purest form of healing and requires the devotion and humility of the medium. This devotion only comes about through one hundred percent trust, hope and faith and presupposes a long-term collaboration between the medium and the spirit world. Here too love is the basis. The combined love of the medium and of the spirit world brings about the cure. This form of cure is known as trance healing. If the medium acts as a channel but remains fully conscious of his actions then the link is still established to its full extent. In this case though the medium largely guides the energy from the world of spirit through his own knowledge. Your scientists have recently proved this. That should not be deemed to be fundamentally wrong. Nevertheless the medium, in this case, does not have a full insight and will therefore work at the material, bodily level or at the symptomatic level. But no cure brought about through the healer's consciousness can last because the underlying cause has not been removed. Therefore the cause, which is to say the focus of the event, retains its ability to influence the patient's energy field. For this reason the disease is not changed, but is simply suppressed and will return. Our healers and experts however can see the real cause and therefore healing in this case takes place at the source of the event.

    Everything is energy and no energy is ever lost. Many healers among you believe that all you have to do is to redirect our positive energy into the patient's energy field in order to bring about a positive outcome. But energy is never lost, which means that now not only our positive energy but also the old negative energy is present. Therefore the cause of the illness continues to exist. On our side of the worlds we transform this energy during trance healing. We do not add new energy; instead we transform the existing energy in a complex process using the body of the medium, whereby the medium also receives a dose of healing energy. This is only possible in a trance. We need another plane of consciousness here in order to complete the process, whereby the depth of the trance is the yardstick for the depth of the cure. We possess the medium's body when they are in a deep trance. From the point of view of your sensory world you would even have to talk in terms of the physical death of the medium. We take over this body and are then even able to undertake physical interventions such as operations or tumour removals. Our healers, specialists and doctors take possession of the medium's body. Others take care of the medium's spirit over here so that the person suffers no harm. Thus many, many hands are employed in bringing about a cure.

Now you will understand that all of this requires a high degree of willingness on the part of the medium to give up his ego and volition, even to forebear the very desire for the patient's recovery, before we can intervene actively. This is the reason we talk in terms of love, humility and devotion. Such a medium spends years in the energy of our presence so that our two worlds can come together and that we can partially physically transform the medium so that this great work can be achieved.

In your time there are only very few who are willing to follow this path, as it will in no way satisfy the ego. The medium is simply the means to an end. This development saddens us greatly. We often wait for years until such a medium is born. Then it frequently takes several decades more until the medium's fate leads him to discover us. The energy of the Christ is and was such a type of energy. My message to you all is that no energy ever departs from the space of creation, whether it was created by human beings or originated in our world. Jesus, the Christ, had achieved the same condition that can only be achieved in trance today whilst remaining fully conscious. But everybody can travel this path. Faith and love alone are capable of opening the path to this new, ancient healing energy. Follow this path. There are so many in our world just waiting to help you. If you could only see the joy among us over a true healing medium then you would not hesitate for a moment. Great things can happen if you believe in this energy.

Respect the trance condition for it is the sacred plane of the priest consciousness and is the plane of transformation. It is on this plane that miracles occur.

Healing

This is where my Lord turned water into wine and made the lame walk again. This is the dimension in which the sacred dance of death, the dissolution of material and the return to the oneness of God takes place. Jesus Christ is the energy through which God expressed his desire for the salvation of all mankind. He is the anointed one, the promised Messiah, who made the healing energy visible to convince all those who still doubted of the greatness of the One. Today you can still feel this energy in the sacristy and in séances when physical phenomena are made manifest through a medium. Healing occurs through the profundity of the connection between our worlds. It takes places in the invisible realm but takes affect in the visible world. These are the transformations and the miracle.

Who is God?

Who is God?

*And Moses said unto God,
Behold, when I come unto the children of Israel,
and shall say unto them, the God of your fathers
hath sent me unto you; and they shall say to me,
what is his name? What shall I say unto them?
And God said unto Moses, I AM THAT I AM: and
he said, thus shalt thou say unto the children of
Israel, I AM hath sent me unto you.
And God said moreover unto Moses, Thus shalt
thou say unto the children of Israel, The LORD
God of your fathers, the God of Abraham, the
God of Isaac, and the God of Jacob, hath sent me
unto you: this is my name for ever, and this is my
memorial unto all generations.*

2 Exodus Chapter 3, Verses 13-15, p. 48

I am the power behind everything. I am the breath of the wind and the love that creates. I am mercy and justice and the knowledge of the universe. I am the memory of time and the cathedral of the worlds. I am that I am. I tell you, you must go! The time has come. My worlds have been apart for two thousand years. Now the time has come for their reunification. Unify the worlds and then mankind will be united. I am the fire of transformation and the ocean of redemption. I am life and death and the voice of truth.

Justice flows from every breath I take and the breath of life flows from my lungs. I am and have been the world, life and creation since the beginning of time. Nothing is unknown to me for nothing happens without my knowledge. Everything was conceived aeons ago and follows the ancient plan of creation. I am the way and the light. Follow me into the light and you will never perish in it nor will you burn. Go, I tell you. Go!

But are we not too small? (A question I asked when I received this message)

What would the ocean be with the droplets, or the wind without the breeze and an embrace without love? Everything is only a tiny part but without this part nothing can exist. The droplet is as big as the ocean and the embrace as great as love and the slightest breeze is like a storm if they are sown at the right place at the right time. No action is ever too small. I see everything, I know everything and I feel everything. Neither the tear nor the breeze nor the embrace happens without my instigation. I have dwelt within you all since the beginning of time and am the energy that feeds the cosmos. I move all worlds for there is only one world. My loving thoughts are the beginning and the birth of your souls and the more you open yourselves to love the greater will be your existence and every action in your world corresponds with an action in the invisible worlds. Acts born of love soar to the realms of knowledge and truth and healing. Acts arising from doubt and base feelings are heavy and are not able to rise up. Your world is heavily burdened with these old energies. Lift up your hearts to the light. Live and breathe in the light. There is never any darkness in the light. Darkness exists below and next to the light. To walk in my light is to be healed. Pass on the light and you shall receive more than you can possibly imagine. Yet nothing new will be added. The essence of everything is already contained within your hearts. Go and proclaim, go and heal, go and speak of my worlds and bring glory into the hearts of mankind. Go … and love. That is all that is needed. A single spark is enough to ignite an all-consuming conflagration. The all-consuming conflagration is the flame of purification and will be brighter than the brightest light. There will be a new star. Its time is nigh and it will shine. Follow this star. It is the way and the truth and will lead you into life. Go.

    Bring back this paradise for mankind. Unite the worlds and be the bridge. Your helpers are many and their name is legion. Darkness will come and engulf you, but you will climb out of the depths and are already carrying the star of light within you and thus will you illuminate the realm of darkness. It is time to return to paradise. Transform the wine of deceit into the water of truth. Let the words flow forth from your hearts and the will inundate the Earth and bring the sacred sustenance to every place on Earth. Every word will be a signal and a sign.

Humility

Humility

I therefore, the prisoner of the Lord, beseech you that ye walk worthy of the vocation wherewith ye are called, with all lowliness and meekness, with long-suffering, forbearing one another in love.

Ephesians Chapter 4, Verses 1-2, p. 792

You have heard the call and want to work as mediums. We welcome this step, however yet another step is required in your development. Whether you will speak or heal as mediums, it is a path of humility and learning throughout the entire journey of your soul. Learning means growth and yet this growth does not mean that you should appear in the guise of new prophets and make people dependent upon you. Travel your path in humility and be less than those who will come to you for help, for they, in reality, are your teachers. Their requests are your challenges. Through them you can either grow or fail.

Pride comes before a fall. This is a realisation from your world and is still as valid as ever. It originates from a saying from Yeshua: „Whatsoever You Have Done to the Least of These, My Children, Assuredly I Tell You, You Have Done It, Even Unto Me." Matthew Chapter 25, 40.

It is not you, who are elevated through your pupils

Humility

but rather your pupils are elevated through you. Never forget this task. To leave people standing in the dark is to be guilty. Serve the light; serve the ascent. Everybody may contribute in his or her own way, the one through healing, another through a positive word that comforts a bleeding heart. Yet others will be the bridge between our worlds. And others again will sing God's praise. Others will give birth to people who will be pioneers. None of you is less than any another. Only the glory of the One towers above all else. You are all travelling the same path. Offer one another your helping hand in humility and help the other to transcend his threshold and barriers so that you too will be helped in your hour of despair.

When you hear the wake up call then follow the track of your heart and the light of your soul. Do not let yourselves be diverted and kneel before the majesty of the Lord, who has prepared this path for each and every one of you. Real greatness is displayed in your actions and not in your words. The way of the medium is a path of service to others for which you will be rewarded and repaid a thousand fold. You will be taken care of if you travel this path of love. Miracles will become possible and limits will be transcended, but remain humble before God and your neighbours, and magnanimous in love. This is the way. Then all the heavens will open to you step-by-step until finally you find yourself looking into the heaven of enlightenment whence we will gently

Humility

collect you. We will bring you home and then you shall know.

Love between Man and Wife

Love between Man and Wife

Note

These final transmissions are actually the first I received at that time. They are not directly related to the development path of a medium and yet they are of such beauty and guide our consciousness back to the concerns of everyday life, which one also has to live to the full. That's why I decided to include them in this publication even though they are not directly related to the subject.

You have journeyed long before you found me. My strength is not great and it saps my energy to appear to you here. My name is Maryam, but I am known under many other names. I live in this lonely, deserted region and have retired into this cave in order to be closer to God and to my partner. My time will come and my time has gone. We were people, bound together in God's will, but we are soul mates for all eternity. They call me the wise woman.

The Bible is full of gaps and arbitrariness and yet it remains the most sacred work. Mankind has been searching for love for two thousand years. We lived it. My master and I experienced perfect love. Listen carefully. In your lives the love between man and wife is limited to the emotional and physical plane. Turn back.

Think of the sacred number three. Only through the union with the spirit, which is holy and sacrosanct, only through the addition of the third element, spirituality between man and wife, can all-embracing love awaken. This will be a love that serves and does not control: a love that will appear as a beacon for others.

Much was removed from the Holy Scriptures so that man and wife can no longer complete the divine unification and the ancient rituals. They have been separated from the union with God. God is love, unconditional, trusting, fertile and always creating. The missing element is spirituality. It is about spirit and ritual. Perform the ancient rituals and your love will be a living prayer. Render homage to your husband and recognise his divinity. He is not and never has been separate from God. Pay homage to your wife and recognise her divinity. She is not and never has been separate from God. Together you are God's children. Like Adam and Eve you have been placed in paradise. Your allotted share is abundance and not deficiency. It was not the serpent that caused your fall but the capriciousness of man. You are still in paradise and you fail to see it. People have planted the message of want in your hearts and have therefore split the Trinity. You became separate and therefore you became seekers. Your banishment was the result of greed and power. God's words are words of love, gentleness and understanding. How then could he be cruel and angry and vengeful? God is love and mercy.

- Learn to see the need in your partner before he sees it himself.
- Learn to touch his spirit to give him confidence.
- Bear him gently and safely over life's obstacles with your love.
- Respect him and believe in him.
- Submit to the divine unity to become one spirit, one body and one blood.
- Be an example and ignite the light of longing in your partner: first comes the yearning then comes the search.
- Love him most when he least deserves it.
- Touch one another, for this is a path to wholeness.
- Comfort your partners in their distress; this is balsam for the soul.

Perfect peace can only manifest itself in the trinity of divine union, namely in faith, hope and love. As long as you have faith and are animated by the Spirit, by spirituality, your love will never die and will never suffer want.

We always talk about dualism. Of course man and wife are opposite poles. And yet both poles represent the truth in equal measure and only through the breath of the holy, inviolable, immaculate and divine spirit can the duality be transformed into an indestructible unity; a unity that is healing and is a balsam for the souls of others. Then it is no longer about differences but about unity. Only in the conjunction between love, passion and spirituality can the divine marriage, which is the wine of life and the breath of immortality, arise. Then two separate beings will become soul mates, with a shared path and a single destiny. Live the ancient rituals and prayers. Sacrifice yourself to the other. Celebrate the union in the knowledge of the divine origin of the other. Recognise in your partner the same light, ignited in their soul, which originated in eternity and will return to it. Then you will remain connected as souls throughout many incarnations. This bond is an eternal bond and is sacred because God wills it to be so.

When did you really see you partner for the last time? Sit opposite one another and look into each other's eyes. Look for the divine spark and the essence of the other in your partner's eyes. See yourselves for what you are; as yearning in human form and as an expression of divine volition; as an instrument designed to spread love on Earth, face to face.

I must leave you now. This place is beyond time and space. We shall meet again and I shall call you again. I bless you and all those with whom you are associated with you.

Now go with God.

The Children

The Children

I send greetings to you all. My heart sings when I see that children mean a lot to you. Children are a gift and they are the seed that you sow. Follow their growth with loving attention and give them wings to fly across life's shoals. Give them sustenance and encouragement and a loving embrace in times of need. They are the reflection of your lives and when you look into the faces of your children you look into your own lives.

- If you discover fear in them then you have sown fear.
- If you discover pain in them then you have sown pain.
- Should your children avoid your gaze then you have sown lies.
- Should the glint in their eyes fade then you have sown darkness.
- Should you discover tears then you have sown bitterness in their hearts.

A childish soul that carries within it the spirit of joy and laughter will become a gleaming reflection of your life. Look into the eyes of a child when it sees the light of the world. The brilliant light of this soul carries the image of eternity within it. Your children are born from the eternal source and have set out on their journey in order to fulfil their destiny. In the eyes of the newborn

The Children

you will catch a glimpse of the glory of the spiritual world. A single look into these eyes will reveal the majesty and miraculousness of creation. You yourselves have become creators in this case. Just as the Father created you in his own image, you have created these tiny little creatures of hope in your own image. But is your own image worthy of replication? Look into the mirror and see your face through the eyes of a child. Is the seed worthy to bear fruit or would it be better for it to shrivel in the dry earth so that no new pain in created? They are born of your spirit and have received the light from the source of light, to which all will one day return.

And yet there are children who lack the nutritional medium of love. Children, who see only pain in a hand and whose souls are waiting in darkness for redemption. Love is the only way to heal these children: hands that cure bleeding hearts and smooth over the scars of the soul; hands that bring comfort in the night and radiate peace and safety; voice that speaks words of comfort in times of fear, and a hand that holds them in firm grip in times of need. Remember you mission and fulfil your destiny. Your children will not travel your road. It is up to you to travel it yourselves. Your children are a reminder of your destiny and they carry the resplendent light of the spiritual world within them.

Acknowledgements

Acknowledgements

These are some of the messages that I have noted down over a long period of time. Some of my pupils convinced me to publish all of this. Perhaps the time has come to do so. There is still so much knowledge from the world of spirit contained within the depths of my computer that can help our souls on our earthly journeys. In taking this step I am gathering all my courage and overcoming my fears. If one single light is ignited in one single person then this step will have been worthwhile.

I would like to thank my spirit guides and above all her from whom this knowledge originates. For many years I did not know who she was and on the day she revealed her identity to me I was filled with incredible astonishment. May she also astonish you.

My thanks also to all of my pupils who put their trust in me; it is lovely to see how your light and the insight within you are beginning to shine. I thank my husband for his unconditional love and care. He is the light of my life. His very existence fills me with quietude and peace. I would also like to thank my parents and my children; they have been my greatest teachers. And I send my love to my grandchildren Melia and Noah and to all those who will come after them. May the radiance in their hearts and the gleam in their eyes never fade; they shine as a beacon in my life.

I thank all the souls in the visible and in the invisible worlds: please continue to be my teachers. And I

Acknowledgements

thank my Creator for this life and for work I have been permitted to undertake.

Finally I would like to allow love itself to speak:

The Song of Songs

The Song of Songs

Though I speak with the tongues of men and of angels, and have not charity, I am become as sounding brass, or a tinkling cymbal.
And though I have the gift of prophecy, and understand all mysteries, and all knowledge; and though I have all faith, so that I could remove mountains, and have not charity, I am nothing.
And though I bestow all my goods to feed the poor, and though I give my body to be burned, and have not charity, it profiteth me nothing.
Charity suffereth long, and is kind; charity envieth not; charity vaunteth not itself, is not puffed up, Doth not behave itself unseemly, seeketh not her own, is not easily provoked, thinketh no evil;
Rejoiceth not in iniquity, but rejoiceth in the truth;
Beareth all things, believeth all things, hopeth all things, endureth all things. Charity never faileth: but whether there be prophecies, they shall fail; whether there be tongues, they shall cease; whether there be knowledge, it shall vanish away. For we know in part, and we prophesy in part. But when that which is perfect is come, then that which is in part shall be done away.
When I was a child, I spake as a child, I understood as a child, I thought as a child: but when I

*became a man, I put away childish things.
For now we see through a glass, darkly; but
then face-to-face: now I know in part; but then
shall I know even as also I am known.*

*And now abideth faith, hope, charity, these
three; but the greatest of these is charity.*

**The Holy Bible, 1 Corinthians Chapter 13,
Verses 1-8, pp. 780-1**

Sources

Sources

Krishnamurti: *Vollkommene Freiheit,*
5. Aufl. Frankfurt am Main: Fischer, 2006, S. 537
ISBN: 3596150671

The King James Bible (1611)

Pistis Sophia, translated by G.R. Mead (2007 [1896]),
Celephaïs Press, Leeds